A WALKING *Testimony*

Stroke Survivor:
MY SECOND CHANCE

By: Antrone "Juice" Moore

and Damien Womack

Health issues can affect anyone, at any age, at any time. There is no such thing as "old people illnesses." The perception is that I'm young and invincible and there's no need to worry about my health. We need to take charge of our health TODAY. Know your family history, it could save your life down the road. Why am I telling you this? Because I suffered trauma to my brain in the form of a massive hemorrhage stroke (Intraventricular and Intracranial) at a young age that I would have never expected to have, and it could have been prevented with awareness. My condition put me in a coma for ten days and rendered me paralyzed and unable to speak, but I made the choice to fight for my health and be here today to share my story. I hope that these words inspire those going through an adverse situation to never give up. Despite my grim diagnosis, I can walk, talk, even run. I suffer daily setbacks, but I don't allow it to damper my spirit. At the end of the day, all that you have is family and faith. My determination and will to get better was fueled by wanting to see my family again. It wasn't easy by any means; I had to work extremely hard. Every day I pushed my boundaries further and trained my body harder; through the pain and fatigue, to get to where I wanted to be. My lifestyle had to change, or I was destined to die young. I'm not a preacher man, just a regular guy with a story to tell. The cards were heavily stacked against me and I beat the odds. If I can do it, you can too. Giving up is not in my vocabulary!

www.whatdoidesire.com

www.juiceexpresseagles.com

Twitter WhatDIDesire

Instagram Whatdoidesire and awalkingtestimonybook

Facebook @whatdoidesirepage and Awalkingtestimony

Table of Contents:

The "A Walking Testimony – Stroke Survivor: My Second Chance" memoir was conceived from my unfortunate encounter with a massive hemorrhage stroke. At the age of 37, I nearly lost my life to a condition that "normally" happens to older folks. I didn't have a clue what a hemorrhage was. It is defined as an escape of blood from a ruptured blood vessel. A stroke is when the blood supply to part of your brain is interrupted or severely reduced, depriving brain tissue of oxygen and nutrients. Within minutes, brain cells begin to die resulting in loss of speech, weakness or paralysis on one side. That's why it's imperative to react quickly to a stroke. Now that I have bored you with the science of what I went through let's get back on track.

My journey to write this book took me from Chicago to Maine to Texas to Michigan to South Carolina to Ohio and numerous stops in between. Every stop benefited me with experience; whether positive or negative. For example, certain destinations were filled with distractions. Other weren't as fruitful with progress, but made up for it with good company.

I spent a lot of hours online, researching the writing process and trying to find people to help. Many doors were closed in my face, but I never gave up. Three, almost four, years later and here we are. I intended to write about the stroke and raise awareness, but as time went on, I realized the way I was carrying on in my life was pertinent to how it happened in the first place. I'm not going to blame anyone but myself for the consequences I have endured as a result of the choices I made.

"Through my trials and tribulations, I put it in your hands. Fighting for my life because of the choices I made. I have no one to blame but myself; a man lost in complete darkness. But through it all, I found the strength to smile."

INTRODUCTION

When I originally envisioned this book, it was simply going to be a memoir on how I survived a massive hemorrhage stroke. But the more I wrote, reflected and questioned, the more the story evolved into sharing my life experiences; experiences that were relevant to how my path lead to my current health issues. We as young people often think that we are invincible; that tomorrow is promised. It goes to show that life is fragile and we can be called Home at any moment.

I've experienced a lot of loss in my short time on this Earth. I have been fortunate and blessed to have received the love and knowledge from the older generation that has come before us. Now, I feel that it is my responsibility to be a leader, a voice, for the younger generation and people with disabilities like me. We as a family have become complacent and have veered off in different directions. My grandmother passed away and a big part of me left with her. She was one of our family's guardian Angels-I truly believe this. We lost pillars in our family. We all know that pillars support structures, without support, the structures crumble.

By writing this book, I hope to bring to light issues that usually go unaddressed in our family; and other families as well. Alcoholism, separatism, and lack of knowledge of family health history are just some of the things I have dealt with in my life. There were numerous occasions where I felt if I had known my family's health history, I could have taken more preventative measures. I feel that I'm one of the chosen ones; surviving an illness that claims more lives than it spares. Miraculously, I received another chance to prove that I have a higher purpose to serve on this Earth. I offer myself as a vessel to mentor the youth in a lost generation. The following events that I'm about to share in this memoir happened pre-stroke, during the ordeal (September 26, 2012) and post-stroke.

Marriage is an institution that is supposed to be between two people, not two people, a college campus and night clubs. My nuptials were built on a foundation of partying. Fresh off of a move from Chicago, I was the hot new face in Shreveport, Louisiana trying to see what the city had to offer. Family is the reason I came to Louisiana; and partially the reason I met my future wife. Like most budding relationships, things started off on a positive note. We went out together, hosted parties and had a great time. Things were casual; we had our own interests and activities. I was still playing basketball and meeting people and she was a registered nurse.

Louisiana State University-Shreveport was right across the street and was fertile with ball players to test my skills against. Making a name for myself on campus increased my notoriety around the city. Parties at my house were crazy! Campus folks, including the LSUS basketball team, residents of the complex, even my wife's co-workers came to party. Our happy home was known around town as the party spot. We had "party favors," drinks, video games and music to entertain our guests. Prior to making my lady an "honest woman," we shared common interests and complimented each other well. Over time, our common ground reaped thoughts of taking our relationship to the next level.

I would send out daily inspirational quotes to close family and friends. My future wife to be responded to my text with, *"Let's get eloped."* Okay, I know what you're thinking…what was your

9

response? Let me tell you, I didn't have a clue what "eloped" meant or was? *"What does eloped mean"* I replied? She told me to get online and look it up. I had to Google the term "eloped" ladies and gentlemen. When I discovered what it meant, I dialed her job and said, *"Are you playing?"* She replied, *"No."* We already lived together, we were comfortable with each other, our relationship seemed unbreakable. *Why are we playing games? Let's stop playing games and make this official.* My grandmother taught me that, as a man, it was my responsibility to ask the woman to marry me. I proposed to her and the rest is history.

Our families did not grant their blessings for us to marry. In hindsight, their reasons were legitimate means for concern. Financially and spiritually, we weren't ready to join our lives in matrimony. People say there are signs that something should or should not happen. If that truly is the case, we ignored each and every one of them! The day before the wedding, my mother and her friend were stranded in Texas at the bus station. They could have missed the wedding because the flight and Greyhound bus departure times didn't correspond. My brother volunteered to pick up my mother from the bus station. I had to accompany my brother for the ride because he hadn't been driving for that long; despite the fact that I had to be at wedding rehearsal. While we are gone, no one bothered to watch the grill that contained the reception food, and the main entrée got burned! My brother is driving like he's trying to qualify for a spot on the Nascar circuit. I'm intoxicated and drifting in and out of consciousness. Travelling in a car at 140 mph with a new driver behind the wheel, across state lines, passing out seemed to be the most inappropriate course of action. To make matters worse, the bride's wedding party was missing a bridesmaid, and we got a call asking to pick her up while we were out. *Are you kidding me?!* I'm the groom, why am I the one running around like a chicken with its head cut off? If I told you everything else that happened, I'd need another book and you'd wonder why I didn't just call the whole thing off.

The wedding day is here and I am running on literally two hours of sleep. Today is the day I join the woman I love in holy matrimony; but, I didn't want to get married any more. *What do I do?* I know, the answer is at the bottom of this bottle of liquor. Apparently, my entire wedding party needed answers and participated. After three hours of searching for answers at the bottoms of bottles and at the end of the blunts (marijuana) we found time to show up to the wedding. Now imagine how you would feel as a bride if the groom and all of the groomsmen were nowhere to be found and the bridesmaids are threatening to leave? To add insult to injury, the guys, when they do show up, are all high and drunk?

The wedding went on as planned, on September 18th 2010, in front of family and associates. According to the storybooks, this should have been the beginning of a happy ending right? I could not have been more wrong. Typically, married couples slow down and focus on each other and building an unbreakable bond. That was far from the case with us.

The party spot kept going strong with new members being added. Beyond a shadow of a doubt, the addition of that piece of paper, the marriage license, was the beginning of the end to our relationship. Marriage should draw us closer and make the relationship stronger. We only succeeded at arguing more, trusting each other less and stressing each other out. Stress can lead to numerous health problems such as diabetes, obesity, asthma, depression and high blood pressure. High blood pressure is a hereditary trait in my family. Couple genetics with a fast lifestyle, not regularly seeing a doctor, unhealthy eating and stress, health issues were inevitable.

The BIG day

We were now newlyweds and things didn't change. The bond between my wife and I should have grown; but instead, the partying increased, the party guest list grew and our marriage was headed down a path of destruction with downhill momentum. Instead of me being the head of my household and taking control of the marriage, I did the total opposite. Two associates continued to stay in our home because they were potentially going to be without a place to stay. I couldn't let them be out on the street; but looking at the overall picture, they were not my responsibility. Little did I know, I left the door open to the devil's playground. *Juice! Juice! Juice! What the hell are you thinking?* My wife was not protected, leaving her to fight the battle of lust and temptation by herself. I vowed to love and cherish my wife and instead I cultivated relationships with everyone else other than with the person who should have been my number one priority. I failed to fulfill my commitment to my marriage and the woman I loved. By allowing all of these extra people to be around so often, I set the table for many of the situations that occurred in our home.

    Going out clubbing and having get-togethers every other day started to take a toll on us as a couple. I can recall a Sunday morning in particular; I was sitting on the couch and a text message came through on my phone that said the magic words, *"Do you want to smoke?"* *"Yes! Of course!"* This particular individual seemed to always be around without the core group. I talked to some guys whose opinions I trust about this particular guy and the consensus was *"Watch this* *mother [expletive deleted] bro, he doesn't have good intentions and has a reputation of sleeping with his friend's ladies."*

The initial episode happened when I went through my wife's phone and read cryptic text messages between her and a friend. They had been conversing about a mystery man. Putting two and two together, I realized that the messages pertained to an individual I knew. With a bottle in hand and the steering wheel in the other, my mission was to locate the man that ruined my marriage. I'm not sure if the fact that I knew this man; one of my groomsman, enhanced the shock. Feeling betrayed and broken, ending his life was the first thought that crossed my mind. I caught wind that he was in my back yard. The plan was to confront this man; this usurper, face to face. This man had the audacity to transgress my marriage, MY WIFE, after all the hospitality! Although I was furious, cooler heads prevailed and I decided the remedy I sought wasn't worth the consequences I'd reap for the rest of my life. My so-called sacred marriage was down the drain. Any attempt to make things right were suppressed by my emotionally charged want for revenge. I immediately sought after an outlet to release this pain. What better place to seek solace than my church?

Please, someone talk to me, console me, reason with me. I arrived at the church and was informed the pastor was unavailable. *The pastor isn't free?!* I couldn't wait! Waiting for the pastor to be free felt like an eternity! My mind was racing; my heart was pounding, and my pastor was busy. If I didn't get help soon, these irrational thoughts will prevail. Standing in front of the church, I dialed my cousin Woodrow's

[Dro] number. Dro was someone that I could lean on during difficult times and vice versa. What better way to deal with an unfavorable situation than with hard liquor? I detoured to the store for a fifth of Hennessy. Sipping straight from the bottle, it was time to go back to my former sanctuary. Operating a vehicle with these thoughts; anger, pain, sadness, in hindsight, was not a good idea. I arrived home and finished the fifth before I got out of the car. Stumbling up the stairs, I recall reciting to myself, *"Lord Forgive me, for I know not what I'm about to do."* With key in hand, I open up the door and immediately feel an intense sensation of rage. I walked directly to the back of the house; to OUR room and sat on OUR bed that was intended for myself and my wife.

My intentions were to confront my wife; *"Why, just why would you do this?"* I needed answers. Hard liquor, heartbreak and charged emotions are a cocktail for disaster. Rage prevailed and an argument ensued. The argument escalated to the point of swearing at each other and nearly getting physical. My wife tried to flee to the bathroom and I wasn't having it. I grabbed for her shoulders, but since I was so intoxicated, I lost my grip and fell back onto the bed. At this point, it was apparent something wasn't right. My wife had run into the bathroom and locked the door as I laid there in tears calling her name. *"I'm not feeling good"* I said through a closed bathroom door. She conversed with me through the crack of the door a few minutes before she finally trusted me enough to come and check on me. Seeing me at the edge of the bed, slumped and resting my head on my arm, she proceeds to take my pulse and check my blood pressure. My wife was an RN, so fortunate for me, I had a professional on the scene.

We didn't own a blood pressure monitor so she says, "Let me run to Wal-Mart. I'll be right back, just lay there." I needed to use the bathroom; after all, I did polish off a fifth of Hennessy. When I got up I felt dizzy, but still tried to make my way to the other room. Right before I got to the toilet, I collapsed and lost consciousness. Unsure of how long I had been unconscious; I awoke to the screams of my wife. *"Juice! Juice! Oh My God Juice!"* I replied, *"I'm okay, I don't know what happened?"*

Conflict turned to concern and I was immediately rushed to the emergency room by my wife. I was disoriented and unable to fill out the paperwork on my own. The nurses aid was working on me and discovered that my blood pressure was through the roof. This was a shock to me; I haven't had any previous health issues. The aid administered some medication to level off my blood pressure and prescribed some blood pressure medicine through my wife's insurance plan. The prescription had to be on her plan because I didn't have any coverage. Fortunate for me, at the time, my wife worked at LSU Hospital; therefore, that loophole allowed for me to be covered. It was a long, quiet ride home.

My mind was racing from a major health scare, and I couldn't get past the fact that one of my groomsmen was laying up with my wife. I went home and took my medication, the first dose of what would be many. The fact that I had to take medication the rest of my

16

life didn't sit well with my spirit. *How did this happen? Why me?* I knew nothing about blood pressure, especially since most of life has been spent being active. Speaking of being active, my activities changed gears to the those of the extra-curricular variety. I started sleeping around with multiple women just because I wasn't thinking logically about the repercussions behind my infidelity. Two wrongs don't make a right, and I was making a bed that there was no coming back from, drowning in my own sin.

We both became very distant towards each other to the point that it got very emotionally draining and I felt lost. Would there be enough love to conquer the hurt and pain that we had caused each other? I was disrespecting the woman I wanted to spend the rest of my life with and continuously committing adultery. At this point I didn't care about anything, not even my own life. It had gotten to the point that I was intentionally trying to end it. The earthly wants and needs coupled with lies and deceit crippled our marriage.

The disease of alcoholism and binge drinking took me down a dark path of misery and pain that no one would want to travel. The best thing to do was separate myself from the one person I once wanted to spend the rest of my life with. I contacted one of my friends, who was also my mentor, and told him I wanted to start coaching. If I could make it back to the sport that I love, maybe I could start putting some positive energy back in to my life. My mentor gave me some contacts and pointed me in the right direction.

At this juncture of my life, I was a functional alcoholic and was trying to run away from my problems. Don't get me wrong, I still loved my wife, but it was obvious that things would not get better until I faced my problem. My true family and friends tried to keep us together but I wasn't trying to hear it! My plan was to leave Shreveport and coach kids; that would get me back on track, so I thought. I told my wife that I was leaving to coach basketball for the youth in Texas. I lead her to believe that I was going to get my life together and move her down there; but deep down I knew I wasn't coming back.

My actions had me feeling that I didn't deserve to be with this woman. My first coaching gig was going to be in Fort Worth, Texas. The so-called plan to improve my life unraveled quickly. The wife was saying I left her; *"I'm going to file for abandonment!"* but that did not deter me from going after this opportunity. Maybe time apart would be good for us? I was promised compensation for coaching this newly formed team, but I came to find that was far from the truth.

A former N.B.A. player was letting me stay with him and his family. Two of my friends would come to help coach as well because they were given the same promise. The three of us decided to make the best of our situation and prove we deserved to be youth coaches. We were willing to do whatever it took to show we were hungry for success. Gym, eat, sleep, repeat. Gym, eat, sleep, repeat. We became gym rats; for hours on end, we trained the kids and hosted tournaments. Parents took notice of the level of passion we had for instructing the kids. Not only were the parents of our players recognizing us, other teams took notice of our ability. Word got out that we weren't being compensated, so some of the parents starting helping out the best way they could. They would slip us a few dollars here and there, or would treat us to a meal. Eventually we got fed up and started to do what we knew best...flirt.

Dealing with the female parents and building a rapport with them would eventually lead to...we will call them "situations". While I'm engaged in these "situations" I was emailing my wife and asking her to send my medication. Our relationship was so disengaged the emails were plastered with hate and animosity, threats of divorce and profanity. My wife continued to taunt and torment me via email saying, *"I'm still sleeping with the enemy, now what you going to do? You chose to leave me now you want to play the victim when I'm the victim?!"* If you have ever seen Rocky IV, the title fight between Ivan and Apollo, you know how devastating the final punch was. *"I'm going to have sex with him for his birthday, we would appreciate if you would not contact us...divorce papers will be in the mail soon."* Talk about a drop the mic and walk off the stage moment. To add additional insult to injury, the same people that were in my circle in Shreveport, the same ones that were partying, smiling, shaking hands, were throwing me under the bus! They were telling my wife about the things that I did, while going the extra mile to embellish the story. *Wow!! Really?!* These so-called friends ridiculing me like I wasn't the one sticking my neck out for them! Karma definitely came full circle. As promised, my wife's cousin called me and told me the divorce papers were sent to my mother's house. I made my way to Chicago to sign the papers and

19

returned to Dallas, Texas. What a triumphant return, no wife and still no income. I was desperately in need of something to fill the void. The conversation I had with my child's mother in Maine would remind me of what that something was.

Basketball. Ball is life. Let me rephrase that, ball was my life. Circumstance and geography didn't allow for me to see my youngest daughter for approximately five years. If I had the financial means, I would send my daughter material things, because I couldn't physically be there. I was an elite basketball player and there were highlights videos and articles available displaying my skills. My youngest daughter was captivated with my highlights and told me she wanted to become a basketball player like me. Saying that I was overjoyed by her decision was an understatement; I was elated! The fact that my youngest child wanted to follow in my footsteps made me a very proud father. Her big sister was already playing basketball for her school in Chicago. Keyanna wanted me to come to Maine to coach her to be one of the best players, like her father.

At the time, I was in Texas coaching someone else's youth team. Why not go to Maine and start my very own youth basketball team? The opportunity to coach my own flesh and blood, and pass on the lessons I learned in life, reenergized my desire to continue on with my dream. Little did I know, this trip to Maine would be the beginning to the biggest change in my life.

Instructing my youngest daughter Keyanna

I had dreams of waking up and seeing my youngest daughter greeting me with *"Good morning daddy"* in that beautiful voice of hers. That dream, however, did not come to fruition because the mother of my child wasn't receptive to the notion like I had hoped she would be. I wanted to mend our broken relationship, but too many years had passed. There were different relationships and even a marriage on my resume. After five years, how many people do you know that would allow you back into their lives; especially when you left them to pick up the broken pieces? Once I was able to accept that a reunion with my child and her mother wasn't feasible, I ended up staying with some players that I had helped get in to school from Chicago that I had built a close relationship with in Maine.

My focus was trying to make things right with my youngest daughter; however, the less than amicable split with my baby mother influenced her to not allow me visitation for weeks at a time. Depriving me of seeing my child was putting me in the ground for sure. I felt as though I had hit rock bottom; continued to get belligerently drunk, and lost my basketball career because of the poor choices I made. Legal troubles limited my capacity to earn income in my profession [at the time]. If you have any pending court issues or owe child support, you are not allowed to leave American soil.

In 2009, I had a try-out in TPBL, the #1 International Summer Pro League, and it didn't go the way I had planned. I never could regroup after that; playing semi-pro basketball making a non-livable wage, I might as well work at Applebee's and coach the kids! If you're not in the NBA or in one of the higher level overseas leagues, you might as well get a regular 9 to 5.

On the night of September 25th, 2012, we had a big party to celebrate my becoming a volunteer youth basketball coach and the opportunity to coach my daughter. Everyone that attended this party brought some type of alcohol, marijuana, and pans of chicken wings. We played cards, listened to music, had a great time with great company. The losing team in cards had to take shots of alcohol. As the night went on I started to feel dizzy. I figured it was me reacting to the plethora of shots I had taken that night. Staggering out of my friend's house at 5 am, knowing that I had to get up at 9:45 am to train some friends, was a bad judgement call.

That morning, I was late getting up. I was awakened by an excruciatingly painful headache and my roommate yelling, *"Get your drunk butt up!"* The thought of going to the gym wasn't attractive and it felt like somebody had hit me in the head multiple times with a baseball bat. Anybody that knows me, is aware that I get up every morning and send out inspirational and/or motivational quotes on Facebook. The messages are intended for my loved ones and people that were lost like myself. Everyone needs to hear encouragement and reassurance from time to time. This particular morning, I wrote *"You will lose someone you can't live without, and your heart will be badly broken, and the bad news is that you never get over the loss of your beloved. But this is also good news. They live forever in your broken heart that doesn't*

23

seal back. And you come through. It's like having a broken leg that never heals perfectly- that's still hurts when the weather gets cold, but you learn to dance with the limp."

Upon arrival to the YMCA, I tried to begin my routine, but I could barely focus and it was hard for me to breathe. My heart was racing so hard, that I could hear it. What is going on with my body? It was unusual, but I chalked it up to lack of sleep and drinking all night. We went to the weight room to start our cardio and chest routine. My body felt like a series of volcano eruptions were going off inside. I was using the elliptical machine and was really feeling dizzy and nauseated. There was not a bead of sweat present on my body. I was completely dry! It was hard for me to breathe, even with fans and the air conditioner going in the facility. I stepped off the elliptical, planted both feet on the ground, with the left foot in front in front of the right. Right foot was working, left foot, not at all. My left side started to drag a few feet away from the elliptical machine; in excruciating pain, I screamed to one of my friends *"I can't move!"* At first, no one took me serious; I could feel my body deteriorating, my motor skills were failing me. After my friend found out it wasn't a joke, he ran over to me, grabbed on to my shoulder and helped me to the gymnasium.

As we entered the gym, I could feel my heart racing even faster. He laid me on the bleachers and the first thing that came to mind was to call the mother of my youngest child, who is currently in the medical field. At the time we weren't seeing eye to eye, but I felt like she would be able to help. I had my friend dial her number and hand me the phone on my right side. She answered and said *"Why are you calling my job drunk Juice, its 10:30 in the morning?!"* and I replied *"What are you talking about? I'm not drunk! I'm in the gym and my head is banging, I'm in trouble!"* My eyes began to roll to the back of my head. The pain was excruciating all I could do was slouch in between the bleachers. As my bodily functions slipped further and further out of my control, it dawned on the mother of my child that these are the symptoms of a stroke. She said to me, *"Hand someone the phone because I can't understand a word you're saying, your words are slurring badly!"* My friend took the phone as I laid my head back down, grimacing in pain. I began to cry when I overheard my friend tell his girlfriend, *"Yo! Call the ambulance!"* She blurts out *"Oh my God, he's having a stroke!"* Hearing the word 'stroke' at such a young age, I didn't know what to think. *Is this how it all ends? Is this my curtain call? The final countdown?* The hospital was only five minutes away from the YMCA so the paramedics arrived on the scene quickly. As I was being loaded on to the stretcher, the guys in the gym surrounded me and with tears in their eyes said *"Juice, it's going to be okay buddy!"* I could feel my body going in to shock and started losing my voice while they were inserting the IV in my arm. During the ambulance ride, I started to fade in and out from the medication they were administering to me. It seemed like it wasn't doing any good because my head was still pounding. I was transported to Maine General Hospital in Augusta, Maine. My body was going haywire; doing things that I couldn't control. All I could hear were the voices of the nurses and doctors that were treating me. Tears streamed down my face when I saw the mother of my child standing over me sobbing. She was holding my hand, comforting me, similar to that of someone comforting a hospice patient whose life is slipping away. This can't be my last day on Earth! I screamed out in tears, *"Make it stop!"* My body and mind are out of sync and like two separate entities. I had to be restrained and doctors injected a medication in to my IV which was intended to induce a coma. My blood pressure was at levels so high it was similar to animals in the wild. Fading from consciousness, I told my baby mother not to tell my family. I couldn't bear the burden of being the source of my family's pain that they were about to endure. Despite my request, I knew that she was going to inform them of what happened; especially because of the severity of this matter. Before I could utter another word, my grip from her hand becomes loose.

My heartbeat was deafening to me like the pounding of a bass drum. My heartrate is decreasing and I start to see flashback of my life. The first image I recalled was of me playing with my youngest daughter flying her kite for her birthday that was the previous week. My chest feels like a vacuum cleaner is sucking all the air out as I'm gasping for air. The feeling was similar to an incident that happened to me when I was 12 years old. My family was sitting on the porch and I had a new bicycle. I thought I was the man and did a wheelie down the block as they cheered me on. My shoelace got caught in the pedal and I fell on my back. Once I connected with that concrete, all of the wind was knocked out of me. If you have ever had the wind knocked out of you, that is exactly what I was feeling at that moment in the hospital. The last words that I can recall are from the nurses, *"Code Blue!"* My brain is shutting down, my mind is blank, thoughts and words are incoherent. I was losing this battle…

Taken less than a week prior to the stroke.

The Cat Scan showed that a blood vessel in my brain had erupted. The doctor at Maine General suggested that my daughter be pulled from school, for this may be the last time she sees her father alive. The odds of my survival was initially predicted at 50/50 by one physician and the other predicted a far more fatal outcome. The options presented to the mother of my child was unacceptable and she opted to contact Maine Medical Center.

Maine General did not have a trauma center at the time; Maine Medical was equipped with a facility and a qualified neurologist. Head neurologist, Dr. Sedar, suggested a procedure for me that was still in the clinical trial stage, called Tissue Plasminogen Activator [TPA]. TPA was administered intravenously with the purpose of dissolving the clot and improving blood flow to the part of the brain being deprived of blood flow; however, there was no guarantee that the drugs would take to my body. My mother asked the doctor *"what if we deny having this procedure done?"* He replied, *"if he doesn't get this treatment, then there is a great possibility that he could die. The leakage of blood of the erupted blood vessel has almost filled to the top of his head and is putting pressure on his brain. We have to drain the fluid so that we can rush him to Maine Medical Center."* The trauma center was almost an hour away, and time was slipping away.

The paramedics rushed me to the medical center while the mother of my child trailed behind. Time was limited and the window of opportunity to save my life was rapidly closing. My spirit started to leave my body; similar to having a dream, but this dream was for an eternity. There would be no tomorrow; nothing but pure darkness…and voices far beyond what I could interpret or comprehend. One was a familiar voice, the voice of my mother was crying out to me, *"You have to fight son! You have to fight for your two daughters that need you, and so do I! Please don't leave us son!"* I screamed as loud as my voice would allow me to, *"Mama! I'm trying to come back"* as I'm looking down at my body and she is holding my hands and crying hysterically. I realized that I was having an out of body experience. Wow! This was something I have seen in movies, but never could I imagine that this would be happening to me. *Wait! How did Mom Dukes get here? Am I about to die? She can't hear me?* I floated towards my mother trying to kiss her but drifted past her into complete silence and darkness.

All of my pain was gone. *Where was I? What happens next?* My time seemingly had expired, its seem to me like I was drifting on a never-ending path. In the distance, I noticed what seemed to be a mansion. Inside, the appearance was similar to a church alter. Silence…pure silence. As strong as I thought I was, the terror was stronger. Is this the place where destruction awaits?! I give it one more try, I called out, *"Jesus, I know I was put on this Earth for a purpose and I hope I served it to your satisfaction. Oh Lord, if I didn't please you, I'm ready to accept the repercussion,"* as I begged for my life. *"Please give me another chance to say my last good byes to my daughters, my mother, and my family"*. As I continued to plead, I started to gag. I heard distant voices, but these voices were distinct and amazing. I drifted towards the voices and noticed a light; the most beautiful light I had ever seen. My vision is blurry but I could see a figure? *It can't be?!* The closer I get, the brighter the light gets. The figure forms into a person I know very well. I began to rejoice, for the figure was my late grandmother, who was called home in 1999. She was as beautiful as she was when she was alive. I was looking at my angel on Earth, but in the afterlife.

Seeing her smile took me back to the five-year old version of me. My grandmother spoke to me. She said, *"Grandma will never leave you. I will always be there even if I'm not here physically."* I drew near my grandma to touch her and the beautiful ray of light reflected off her body and she began to drift away. *"Grandma!"* I screamed with what seemed to be a river of tears flowing from eyes. *"Please let me go with you, I have missed you so much! Please don't leave me here in this mansion!"* Grandma replied in a heavenly voice, *"Nick don't let go. Hold on grandson, don't let go of life. Your princesses, your mother and the family…they need you more than I do, and it is not your time."* At that moment, I started to feel my spirit draw into a light. As I drift through what appeared to be a tunnel, I started to hear the flat line sound coming from the monitor. My spirit re-entered my body and my heart was beating at a steady pace. My eyes opened to an entire room of clapping people similar to if I were in an arena and hit the winning shot in the playoffs; except the ovation from the crowd was replaced by the nurses in the ward. Tears fell from my eyes and I was in disbelief and confused. I pleaded for one last chance to say goodbye and I got my wish. This was a sign that there was a greater plan for me.

I was hooked up to numerous machines; approximately 80 wires, tubes and needles attached to me running from my brain down to my groin area. With all these extra attachments, I looked like a cyborg on an episode of Star Trek; only this was reality. Imagine transforming from a premier athlete to nearly a vegetable. I was unable to move my limbs and I could only answer questions with nods and head shakes. I know I asked to come back, but not like this. Reflecting on this era of my life, I feel ungrateful for complaining about my physical shortcomings. The big picture of being granted a second chance was lost in the "woe-as-me" mentality. The coma and ICU stay lasted ten days before I was admitted to general floor. Due to financial constraints, my mother had to leave. While I was asleep, she returned home. When I opened my eyes and asked *"Where is my mother?"* my baby mother replied, *"She's gone back to Chicago."* Tears immediately welled up in my eyes. Half of my support system was gone and I missed her. I was still deeply immersed in my medical crisis.

Paralysis is a condition that I wouldn't wish on my worst enemy. It's similar to being a baby; you evolve and grow to a toddler, learning and developing along the way. Learning everything all over again had to be one of THE hardest experiences of my life. Thinking back on my struggle to execute the most basic functions in life; walking, talking, holding a conversation-the things we take for granted-brings tears to my eyes. It was difficult to converse with my children, that were eleven and seven at the time. Your children can't understand your struggle because you can't even explain it to them. Many days and nights, I would lie in bed staring at the wall. Severely depressed and feeling worthless I began to feel that my life had no significant meaning. I prayed, day and night for clarity, guidance and healing. The nurses and doctors were tremendous with helping me cope with my illness. There were days that I had to will my way out of bed. My body was weak and aching. Dealing with the loss of my motor and interpretation skills was extremely frustrating. The only thing that I had was my faith. I had to keep the faith. It's extremely difficult to stay positive when you are constantly bombarded with family and friends that are stuck in shock and disbelief over my condition. Meanwhile, I am the one actually living this nightmare. I didn't know how to deal with it at first. I didn't want to face the world; the hospital was my sanctuary that I never wanted to leave.

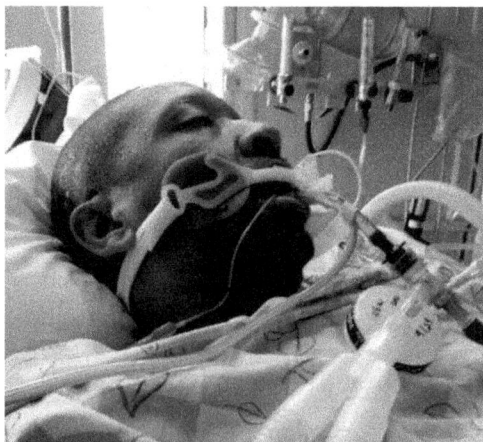

These machines kept me alive during my coma.

32

Although I was on the road to recovery, some of my days were a blur because I was heavily medicated. The side effects of the medications made it so that I was unable to do much for myself outside of answer questions with a nod or head shake. In order to get me out of bed they had to elevate me with a harness- a.k.a. jack-that hurt my scrotum so bad it brought tears to my eyes. I couldn't speak so my only forms of communication to let them know that these machines were hurting me were to cry or wince in pain. There were numerous occasions my mother and baby mother paid me a visit and I had no idea that they were even in the room. When I was finally able to verbally communicate, some of the things that came out of my mouth either didn't make sense or were borderline hysterical. The staff was giving me the drugs to calm me down, but in hindsight, the treatment was ineffective.

That entire year the doctors that put me in the [TPA] clinical trial tracked my progress. A series of tests were run to show how the medication worked on me in comparison to other's around the world participating in the trial. Vaguely, I remember being transferred from the ICU to a regular room and they were videotaping me. The meds had me so discombobulated I couldn't figure out why I was on camera. There was a new doctor and nurse in my room explaining to me how I got into the trial in the first place. My mother consented to my participation in the trial, which also approved consent to be questioned and recorded. I would go on to be recorded three times by the TPA trial interviewers over the course of the year. The initial interview I can barely remember. I was still feeling the effects of the numerous medications in my system and was fresh from being disconnected from all of the machines. Around four months after the first TPA interview, Kennebec Journal Newspaper ran an article on me. There were some inaccuracies in the article and I took criticism for it. The amount of time spent in a coma and in the hospital were misrepresented and some people took it as me sensationalizing the story; when in fact, it was an honest mistake from someone still recovering from a major brain trauma. Two months after the newspaper article, I would participate in my second TPA interview, but with improved cognitive response. The third and final interview was towards the end of the year. It wasn't until a year after that I found out from my primary physician what medications were going into my system. I was so hurt and confused when I learned this information. My family had no idea of what the long-term effects of these drugs were and what type of lasting effects they would have on me.

Being on nine different medications during the TPA trial distorted reality. The hospital was like another world. Every day activities such as watching television were scary events. I could see a fire on the local news and I would truly believe I was in Hell-just from seeing an image of fire! The images on the screen were the aftermath of Hurricane Sandy's destruction. Floundering interpretation skills coupled with the side effects of the medications had me hallucinating and thinking crazy thoughts. All of a sudden, the nurses were out to get me and a high profile entertainer in the music industry was trying to sleep with my youngest daughter. The thought wasn't absurd because a celebrity could be attracted to my daughter, the crazy part was that she was only eight at the time.

I wasn't aware that the doctors increased my doses of medication. The meds made me sleep like I was a hibernating bear. The people that were visiting me faithfully were inconvenienced by the fact that each time they stopped in to see me, I was looking at the back of my eyelids. My loved ones requested two things: 1. Take me off some of the medications 2. transfer me to Thayer Hospital to get closer to my youngest daughter Keke.

The road to recovery was paved with intense occupational and physical therapy. I had my work cut out for me, I still couldn't walk or eat without a feeding tube. I needed a machine to monitor my intake of the necessary calcium and vitamins because I couldn't eat table food. I lost a lot of weight because I was basically on a liquid diet. Using the restroom required a nurse to hold a container while I filled it. Thayer Hospital was my stepping stone to gaining strength and trying to return to some semblance of normalcy.

My moment of weakness came when the mother of my child came in and asked me, "*Juice do you know the date and how long you been in the hospital?*" I didn't understand the question until she showed me the pictures of my stay in the ICU. The pictures served as a reminder of how far I had come. Instantly, my emotions overcame me and I instantly started sobbing. She also said told me that I was in a coma. It had been over a month since I looked in the mirror. The man in the mirror was not me. The reflection was of a man with a full beard and unkempt hair. Talk about feeling helpless and ugly. The next morning, I got a roommate that would change my life. He was an older man that had suffered two heart attacks. What made this man memorable was his loud and up front personality. He was nice to me from day one; had my back like a life-long friend-not so much to the nurses and therapist, he was very grumpy to them. Despite my roommate's "Mr. Grinch" like personality; our room became a popular destination for visits from the staff.

I was determined to learn how to maneuver my body on my own. A part of my therapy was to roll my body and come up on my elbows to help push me to the edge of the bed and sit in an upright position before being helped to the restroom. My personal therapy sessions were going great until I got the bright idea to try to get up without assistance in the middle of the night. Nature called and I had to eliminate [many of us call this a number two]. Needless to say, I wasn't quite ready to attempt this on my own. I rolled over to my right side and got to the edge of the bed like usual. Lifted the bed up with the control, attempted to stand up with the slippery hospital footies on my feet and BOOM, fell on my naked butt. My legs were facing the heavens, with nothing but a gown on. The only place for the doo-doo to go was everywhere. The nurses rushed in to my den of shame with the alarm going off from the bed that was so loud that you would have thought you were on an army base. *"Juice what were you thinking?!"* yelled the nurses coming from everywhere. Waking up the whole unit on the floor. *"Never do that again you could have hurt yourself!"* I was so embarrassed! I felt like the puppy that gets its face pushed in poo when it goes potty inside of the house. The only thing I could say was, *"I'm so sorry, please don't tell anyone"* as I was crying like a big baby. I'm sure my incident is a legendary lunch room tale now.

The following morning, I was awakened by the enforcer of Thayer Hospital, code-named "Sargent Slaughter (Jeanne)." The 'Sarge' was one of two people I dreaded seeing, along with "Vinnie the Exterminator." Those two would push me to the limit and beyond. Attempts to dodge them were futile. They knew where to find me and that they would eventually catch me. One of the nurses, Stacey, nicknamed me 'Sally' because I would complain about the difficulty of the rehab. She saw so much potential in me and wouldn't let me charm my way out of therapy like I could with the other staff members. In hindsight, the staff had to push me hard, in order to push me out the door and back in to the real world. Not having insurance will punch your ticket out the door much quicker.

Bottom line, I was a [financial] strain to the bottom line. A month had passed and I was still laboring to walk 200 feet. My youngest daughter Keyanna knew I was sick, but was not accepting it as an excuse for me to not try. *"Daddy get out of that chair and play with me!"* Choking back tears I replied, "Daddy can't right now," the disappointment seared deep in my soul as I embraced her and she laid her head on my shoulder. I couldn't take it any longer and I asked my princess to push me outside. My anxiety was through the roof, for I hadn't been outside of the hospital walls since I was transferred from Maine Medical Center to Thayer. Focusing my gaze on my daughter, so many questions swirled around in my mind. *"Would I ever be able to push her in a swing?" "Will I ever be able to play with her?"* Truth is, I can barely stand, let alone even think about playing with a seven and eleven-year old. The thought burned more than the after effect of a shot to my stomach and everyone knew I hated shots.

My hospital charts specifically said," He doesn't like needles." Little did I know, needles were going to be the least of my worries. The week of Thanksgiving I was told by the mother of my child that I was going to visit Chicago; what she failed to tell me was the trip was permanent. Physically and mentally I was not ready to journey out in to the world that is now unknown to me. I'm disabled-a nearly immobile man in a mobile world. I was leaving my roommate, whom I had grown extremely close to. My nurses were in tears and didn't want to see me go. Two months of visitation with my child and the mother of my child was coming to an end. I had become accustomed to seeing them and my feelings for her were rekindled. Maybe we could get back together, give it another chance?

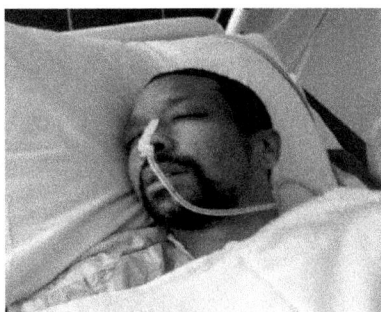

Hooked up to the feeding tube

38

At first I could not comprehend why she told me that my trip was a vacation. Reading between the lines, she was trying to shield me from the fact that she was cutting ties with me. I was blind to the fact that she was there to pick me up because I was being discharged. The thing that I knew for sure was this was the initial step in re-assimilating myself back into society.

This day would be my first attempt to exit a car since the stroke. Just getting out of the car was an ordeal. Of course I practiced with the occupational and physical therapists at the hospital, but this was live action. Equipped with my walker, I had to make my way from the car to the stairs. The driveway was made of rocks and that of course, had me moving like a newborn doe-a 6'3" Bambi. If maneuvering over rocks was this hard, how was I going to catch two planes and get through Chicago O'Hare Airport with a duffle bag and walker?! Thank goodness the airline had a caring staff and motorized carts to assist me. The carts could only take me so far; therefore, I had to lumber the rest of the way on my own. My uncles Tommy and Leon met me halfway to baggage claim and helped me down the stairs. The walk was short, but it felt like a lot of long, painful miles. The look in my uncles' eyes showed how much they didn't recognize their nephew. The energetic, jovial Juice was now a sluggish shell of myself.

There was no amount of therapy that could prepare me for what I was about to face… my Chicago family! <Cue the dramatic music here.> We as a family have always been dysfunctional. Every

39

family has their shortcomings, but at the end of the day, family is all we had. The destination was my mother's house. I was in a lot of pain, but did not want to show it. My upbringing was tough and taught me to exhibit a tough persona. In the back of my mind, I felt my family wouldn't accept me for how I looked now. Sure enough, when I arrived at the house, you would have thought I had a growth on my face. My family members were accustomed to my original appearance and now I looked like a "cancer patient" to them. I thought that my condition would garner a little more compassion and affection from my mom, but I was only partially right. My mom and I have the type of relationship that many people wouldn't understand. There are still times that I don't understand it.

Going through that out of body experience helped me formulate a different perspective. It may sound crazy, but I am forever grateful for that 10 days I was in a coma. The experience showed me how life would be without my mother and my mother had the opportunity to see how life would be without her only child. We sometimes take for granted the time that we have with our loved ones. I know in my heart that my mother wants what's best for me, but sometimes I just want her to show it. The emotional void that I felt was filled by my aunt and grandmother. Everything went back to "normal" my first day back from the hospital.

My mother and I had a disagreement over one of my long-time girlfriends coming to visit. It wasn't so much the fact that I was freshly out of the hospital and should wait to have visitors; it was more so because of my mother's feelings towards my female companions. Ever since I was a little boy, my mother never liked any of my female friends. When she made my friend leave, we got in to an argument. In order to diffuse the argument, I took my walker and trekked two blocks to the laundromat. All I could do is sit there in tears and try to calm down. I hadn't been home for a full day and we were already back to our old ways. Eventually, my uncle came and picked me up from the laundromat and brought me home. When I got home I didn't know what to expect. I was bracing for another possible confrontation, but I was met with love and acceptance from my first shining star-my oldest daughter. The best part of my day was receiving a kiss and warm embrace from my beautiful Takila (a.k.a. "Pooh Bear"). I finally got to sit down and talk to her about what I had been missing for two months. We talked until the medications overcame me and I drifted off to sleep.

Thanksgiving Day was the next morning and we were going to my aunt and uncle's house to see family for the first time, post trauma. The ride from the south side of Chicago to Waukegan was about an hour. Everyone was anticipating my arrival since the "miracle baby" was making an appearance to dinner. That's the nickname my mother gave me when I was in the hospital. I wasn't supposed to make it, and I beat the odds.

We arrived to our destination and my daughter tried to give me my walker. I refused to use it, I had something to prove! My gait was slow, but I took it one step at a time. Pooh helped me to the living room chair and I was greeted with bear hugs. It was amazing to be around family but the vibe felt different. I was used to being treated like "Juice," not like someone you would visit in hospice. I'll never forget the looks of sorrow and disbelief my family gave me. The former version of me would have been all over the house, laughing, joking, livening up the place. Instead, I was sitting in this chair watching the older folks argue about past events, while the younger generation was upstairs turning up [having a good time for those that aren't hip to this term]. If I were more foolish, I would attempt to climb those steep stairs just to escape the negativity. Luckily, my cousin, Woodrow [Dro], had my back and volunteered to help me up the stairs.

Dro was more like a brother rather than a cousin. He was the only family member to come to every one of my basketball games in Chicago. We were only five years apart, and we had a lot in common. He came downstairs and said, *"Come on bro I'll help you upstairs."* My mother looks on as my face is grimacing in pain and replies *"uh uh" he is too weak to walk up those steep stairs!"* Dro had a smile that was infectious and charming. He flashed that smile that not even the slickest car salesman could match and replied, *"Auntie, I got this, I will help him upstairs."* Dro lead me up the stairs and I immediately heard the sounds of joy and laughter. Now this is what Thanksgiving should feel like with the younger generation! That bickering and fighting from the older generation down stairs was for the birds!

Life in Chicago presented numerous obstacles. I needed to continue rehab, but I didn't have any benefits. Thirteen medications and the lack of insurance made the bills hefty; especially since I was going to be on meds the rest of my life. My attempts to gain disability were denied four times in three months. My parents were footing the bill and I was starting to feel like a financial burden to them. I had to do something, so I decided to call my Maine family and asked if I could come live with them. They agreed to take me in and I had to put the situation in Chicago behind me. It was just a matter of the when's and how's to get there.

Not being able to get along with my mother like we should hurts me to my core-I still love her unconditionally despite everything. Although the return to Chicago didn't go the way I wanted, it wasn't all bad. I was able to see my biological father, Howard Moore Sr. for the first time since my stroke. Seeing what my pops had been through and overcame was such an inspiration. My father suffered not one, but two strokes. He is the strongest man I know and he is my hero. A son needs a father to look up to, but because of the choices I made, we shared the same predicament. I valued every moment that I spent with him because our time is limited. Once you have a stroke, you are more susceptible to it happening again. Even with my father's condition, his personality shined through. My father, being the jokester that he is, had me, my mother and Pooh laughing all night. Why weren't there more of these moments?

The following day would prove to be bittersweet. This would be the day that I would be able to visit one of my favorites uncles, Tyrone 'Spanky' Williams. Uncle Spanky is currently serving a life sentence without parole in Joliet Correctional Prison for a crime he didn't commit. The procedures the facility used to check us in were very unpleasant, especially with how weak I was. Anyone that has watched television about prison knows that the guards check you for contraband. Once we got past the hound dogs, I finally was on my way to see my uncle. Due to prison regulations, my walker was not allowed because it was considered a weapon. Without that walker, I had to struggle down the stairs because of my body's weakness. Pooh Bear and my mother braced me while I held the railing. When we finally got to the visitation area, Uncle Spanky could not contain his excitement.

What made this visit so special was the fact that he hadn't seen Pooh since she was a little girl. We talked for a while, and as he had done all of my life, he offered me some good advice. I could tell my physical deficiencies didn't change how he felt about me. With a smile on his face he said, *"Don't let this get you down. You're strong, don't lose your purpose nephew. Continue your journey, this is a minor setback for a major comeback. I bet you still a monster on that court!"* My reply was, *"The best is yet to come, you will see Uncle Spanky."* Since it was a weekday, the visit had to conclude after two hours. Leaving my uncle, knowing that he has to go back to a cell and I get to walk out free, was the hardest thing to do.

New Year's Eve would be a very solemn time for me. Because of the altercation that took place on Thanksgiving, no one wanted to come visit and were in different directions. Feeling depressed, I felt that I had overstayed my welcome. I called my pops and asked him to get me a ticket to leave Chicago. Shortly after the New Year, I was on a plane leaving Chicago and headed to Maine.

My father, Howard Moore Sr., Pooh and I

45

Even though I didn't want to leave Pooh Bear and my mom and pops, I had to begin a new journey. It was still a struggle for me to walk and comprehend basic everyday duties. The Peaslee family took me into their home without a dime in my pocket and a bag of clothes. The first order of business was to acquire health insurance. I went to the city hall of Augusta, Maine and received assistance with my medicine. The next pressing matter I had to deal with were my medical bills. My month stay in Thayer Hospital was upwards of a few hundred thousand dollars! *How was I supposed to pay that back, and especially with no income?!*

Before I left City Hall, the clerk handed me a business card and told me to call the number. The organization on the card was Maine Care Partners. They were instrumental in helping me get my life moving in the right direction. I spoke with Mrs. Varney, who is the Care Manager of Maine Care Partners, and I explained to her I had been denied disability benefits four times in Chicago. We set up an appointment and she helped me fill out the paperwork. A few weeks later, I was in front of a Social Security Administration board for an examination to determine if I was eligible for disability benefits. I had to undergo a series of tests to determine my mental state. Approximately a month later, a SSA rep called and interviewed me for twenty minutes. I was tense with anticipation on whether or not I would be eligible or denied yet again. *"You will be compensated dating back to when you filed in Chicago and your monthly check will follow,"* she said. I was overcome with joy and called Mrs. Varney to tell her the good news.

My good fortune would continue, I found out during this phone call that I was also receiving a scholarship to the YMCA to rehab. Watching my daughter Keyanna play basketball at the Buker Community Center made me realize that the volunteer coach did not have sufficient knowledge of the game. I had to get back on the sidelines and show my daughter how it's done. My body was weak and I couldn't stand for long periods of time, but I was willing to work hard and do whatever it took to coach my daughter. The next day, with the help of Maine Care Partners, I received a scholarship from Kennebec YMCA. This was the time to strengthen my body and take control of my own destiny.

When I started my own therapy, I trained hard out the gate. My occupational and physical therapy were split up in to two, one hour and fifteen minute sessions. What separates me from most stroke victims? My drive. I refused to just accept laying around and being disabled. I knew anything was possible as long as I put my mind to it and work behind it. If I wasn't doing therapy at Maine General, I was at the YMCA. This stroke was no longer going to be a source of excuses, it was my motivation to go the extra mile. The doctors didn't tell me to do two-a-days, I did that under my own accord. In order to get better, I had to know no boundaries.

I talked to a good friend of mine who was a sports writer for the Kennebec Journal newspaper. This individual followed my playing career through college and was someone I could trust to get the word out about what I was trying to do to help the kids in the community. By interviewing with my friend, a lot of avenues were opened up for me. People contacted me on social media and suggested doing my story as a documentary. The world needed to know how I beat the odds and overcame a massive hemorrhage stroke. I am so grateful that I was able to stay active in the church and work out, but many did not see the depression and loneliness that I endured. Friends and associates started to fall off because of my physical deficiencies-I had become a burden. It goes to show that no matter how long you know someone, if they no longer have a use for you, they will leave you behind. I wasn't bitter; it served as motivation to face any and all challenges.

If I wasn't at the gym, or at close family or friends' home, I was with the one person who mattered the most, Keke. She would come to see me every day after school and made me realize that I had to narrow my focus to create the shortest distance to my recovery. It was a hard pill to swallow knowing that I could work my tail off and never get back to where I wanted to be...

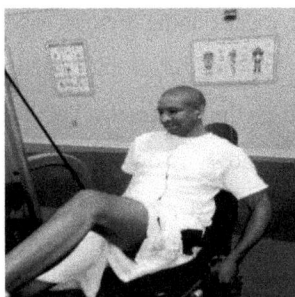

Working hard at rehab
48

My dream finally came to fruition in 2013 by hosting the 'Taking It to the Rim' youth basketball clinic; and later that year, the first Juice Express All Star Basketball game. I was fortunate enough to be recognized by the City Council and Mayor of Augusta, Maine for the impact I was having on the community. I was even able to speak on local cable Channel 7 about what I was trying to accomplish. The positive feedback from such influential people in the community made me want to do more.

In order to honor my auntie and grandmother that passed away from breast and terminal cancer, I did volunteer work associated with their illnesses and also became an advocate for educating people on the signs of a stroke. During this time, I was working on a documentary and running my second Juice Express Basketball clinic. I decided to leave Maine in November of 2013 to go to Atlanta, right around the time of my sister E'lonah's birthday. My sis introduced me to a lot of people she knew around Atlanta, because she was a popular emcee in the club scene; therefore, she had some good contacts. Not only was she an emcee, she also was trying to launch a line of hair products and start her own salon. The most impressive part was; she was doing all of these things while raising her six kids. I can only imagine where our visions would be if we had the financial support to fully pursue our endeavors.

When you want something bad enough, sometimes you have to take risks. Unfortunately, this risk did not reap a reward. Individuals

49

that were big in the industry said that they could see my vision and would help. I got a rude awakening when my phone calls and emails were met with no response. I learned that although you have a great story, not everyone is willing to hear it. Everything comes with a price and you have to have a great support group that believes in your vision to help get where you need to be. In order for me to succeed, I had to be ready for the fast life mentally and physically, and I wasn't quite there yet.

I took up residence in Stone Mountain, Georgia, on the outskirts of Atlanta. By this time, my paid therapy sessions-my primary means of staying active-had dried up. If anything, I needed to stay active so that my muscles would not atrophy and make it extremely difficult-and painful-to get around. My house was located in a hilly neighborhood so I started walking. This was a tall task, especially for someone with my medical condition, but giving up was not in my vocabulary.

Funds were running short and I needed to generate some income. *So how was I going to do that? I know, what I do best*-teach the kids the game that I love. Things did not go as planned for me in Atlanta. I was the new "hot shot" with a lot of knowledge of the game and I was perceived as a threat to those already established in the area. In a strange way, it felt like a turf war. Just because you play the sport of basketball does not mean that you can effectively teach others how to play. Coaching can be a very difficult job, and now that I have been involved in the profession, I empathize with what my coaches went through when I was coming up playing basketball.

'Sis' E'Lonah and I in Atlanta

Even the most positive person can get down and the days were starting to wear on me mentally. I went through a period of feeling depressed which peaked when I found out via social media that I was still married-Memorial Day of 2014-which indeed made this day memorable. The next day, I called the court house to confirm the news because this had to be a joke. It was not… I went off the grid and didn't speak to my supposed ex-wife for weeks. First, my wife contacted my mother and claimed that I wouldn't have been in the hospital if I had been taking my blood pressure medication. I didn't have insurance and couldn't afford it. Second, she didn't even come to what could have been my deathbed to visit. *Why wouldn't you come see your husband if he's in ICU? Did she hate me that much?* If the roles were reversed, I would not have let her die without me being by her side, no matter what.

My sleep patterns were off for months. I had moved on with my life, or so I thought, when I had signed the decree for the divorce. The woman I was involved with at the time did not welcome this news. Our relationship ended because she thought that I lied and knew the whole time that I was still married. The fact that I am still legally bound to my wife held me back from cultivating meaningful relationships. It is a lot to expect of a person to be understanding of my situation. Again, I made the choices that I did and have to deal with the repercussions.

Love is one crazy emotion. Regardless of all the wrong-doing (by both parties), misunderstandings and disagreements, I still loved my wife. Although my feelings were hurt by the fact that she wasn't there when I was in hospital, I couldn't shake the fact that I still wanted to do the right thing and work it out. Even though two years had passed since we were together, I wanted to make it right with my wife. The last time I laid eyes on her was in January of 2012. Somewhere along the way I started to lose motivation. My life was taking a turn for the worse and I needed to get back on track.

My birthday was coming up so I decided to throw myself a birthday party to try and cope with the mental anguish I was going through. So I invited one of my closest friends in Texas (MzThundaKat) and my best friend (Dro) from Chicago to come celebrate with me. It just so happened that all three of us were Leo's with birthdays that were within two weeks of each other. I was in Atlanta-a city rich with culture and nightlife-it was the perfect scenario.

Coincidentally, it was around this time, I was corresponding on Facebook with and getting to know a cousin in Macon, GA whom I had never met before-Gamalia a.k.a. "Mel." I invited him to my birthday celebration and he accepted. When Mel arrived to the party I was fully engaged in festivities for some time and didn't recognize him. Because of my intoxication, he looked like a cross-breed between a Chinese and Arab couple, as opposed to an African-American male. I asked him, "*Are you the help*?" I was ready for another drink and the wait staff was here to accommodate. The music was so loud and I couldn't hear what he was saying so we ended up leaving the club-no one was in their right mind. Mel drove an hour and a half to meet me that night and I'll never forget that.

The next morning, everyone was leaving and my mental meltdown came to a head. I thought seeing familiar faces would help-it made my situation worst. Mel stepped in and showed he was a true family member. He picked me up and took me out for my birthday and we have been close ever since. I love him to death for what he did for me-and it helps that when I'm with him all we do is laugh. Although my landlord was a terrific woman and the people in the house were cool, there was so much that was missing in my life. I tried to suppress the feelings deep down but my past kept surfacing over and over again-it was haunting me. Then one day, I received an email from a parent-Sarah-who was looking for me that kick-started my interest in returning to Maine.

Sarah didn't know that I had relocated to Atlanta and was wondering when my next Juice Express clinic was going to be. She went on saying that my coaching technique was unique and her son Brian learned so much from me. September of 2014 was the perfect opportunity to finish what I started. It was close to my youngest daughter's birthday, so this was a perfect opportunity for me to surprise her. Her mother didn't exactly welcome me with open arms, so I didn't get to see my daughter on her birthday. Undeterred, I decided to take matters into my own hands and I went up to her school the next day and brought the surprise to her. She was so thrilled, she threw her arms around me and almost tackled me to the ground! This was the beginning of a positive turnaround in my life…or so I thought.

Birthday Surprise. She will always be a daddy's girl.

For two months, I was training kids from Blue Wave, an AAU basketball team, thanks to my friend Coach Robert Pilsbury in Portland, Maine. Monday through Wednesday, I would stay with longtime friends Jennifer and Fredrick Evans; on Thursday through Sunday, I would return to Augusta and train kids until the season started at Buker Community Center. Volunteer coaching 3rd and 4th grade opened the door to what would become my AAU team, the Juice Express Eagles. The team was 5th through 8th grade boys and girls. What a dream come true! This was something I had envisioned before I had the stroke. I made a little piece of history, being the first AAU youth basketball team run by a disabled African American in Augusta, Maine.

Playing exhibition games against my longtime friend from Chicago, Nathaniel Ramone Jones' team, who was just as experienced as Coach Pils' team. Their teams were more experienced, so my players were not yet to their skill level. Teams that have players that have been playing together for a while are more fluent and cohesive as a unit. From a competitive standpoint it was a great opportunity because I love being the underdog. Just when it seemed like things were going good, the month of April in 2015 changed my whole perception.

My little cousin, Martell (Dro's son) was murdered as a result of gang violence in Chicago. The following week, a life-long friend of the family (Uncle Mike) was struck by a hit and run driver on his bike. Both deaths ended up being classified as cold cases. Dro and I had a conversation on the phone, I'll never forget the pain in his voice. *"Ice* (Dro's nickname for me was 'Ice Pack') *I will never be the same."* He didn't have to say another word; I knew I had to make it there before the end of the week to attend the funeral.

My finances were almost in the red, but I had to make it to support my family during this tragic time. I caught a flight out of Boston and I was on my way. Imagine losing one of your kids, it's a parent's worst nightmare. All that I could do is offer my condolences and support. I stayed by his side the entire time. He was unusually calm, cool and collected given the circumstances. We as a family were dealing with two losses but keeping Dro strong was my focal point. I think the reality of never seeing his son again set in the next morning and he broke down in my arms. *"Where did I go wrong Ice*?!" he said crying hard. I replied, *"God called your son home Dro, you didn't do anything wrong. He is in a better place than we are right now, it was just his time." I find it strange that we always seem to say this when consoling someone that is grieving, when in reality we have no idea where they are or even if it is a better place.* As I'm consoling him, my mother charges in and says, "Turn off my lights!" I think I stepped outside of myself at this point because I went off on my mother, and in the black community, you don't disrespect your parents. We will call it another "out of body experience" because I lost my temper like someone flipped a switch. I kept repeating myself, *"Are you serious right now?! He just lost his last living son!"* I was so angry, I was in tears. My mother made her way back to her room and shut the door on me and that was the end that verbal altercation.

The next morning, I had to head back to Maine. If you know anything about being kicked while you're down, this was a prime example. My landlord approached me and handed me an envelope. This was very unusual because we always spoke…but she didn't say a word, she just walked away. I went upstairs to get some rest from the long trip home. I went in to my room and noticed there were some things missing in my room. What was going on? I looked down at the envelope and opened it. It was an eviction notice. We all had 30 days to find a new place because we had violated too many of the contract rules. I was only gone a week and things started to crumble at home. A whirlwind of thoughts was in my head, what was going to be my next move? I promised my loved ones that I would reach for greatness and I couldn't stop because of a setback.

I was working on setting up the 2nd annual Juice Express All-Star charity basketball game while still trying to spread the word about my story. The hits kept coming; and without a place to live, I started staying with close friends. Enough time had elapsed of sleeping on couches and in guest rooms to declare myself homeless. There were three people that have always been in my corner financially, Dan, Sarah, and Jerald, that were generous enough to put me up in hotels on occasion to try and keep me in Maine. Despite all of my personal problems, it never stopped being about the kids. I continued to train the kids, making sure their games went on as scheduled and still fulfilled my paternal duties to my daughter Keke. I picked her up every day after school and helped her with homework. Trying to keep up with everything was putting a strain on my health. My blood pressure had risen drastically, but I didn't tell anyone. The only thing they could do is offer me advice. *"Get some rest and take your medication,"* they would say. I already knew I needed to do that, but I had a lot on my plate, but no one could tell because I was always smiling through the storm.

I was told by my oldest daughter, Pooh, I would not be getting a ticket to her graduation. Because of my financial instability, neither one of my children's mothers has considered me a good father. I would think that with my health condition they would be a little more understanding. Regardless of what was going on between me and her mother, I was going to be there for my daughter. I was going to do whatever it took to get to the graduation, even if it meant spending the last dollar in my pocket.

Sleeping on couches wasn't always comfortable, but something I had to do.

Martell and Dro

Martell's funeral

I talked to some friends from Maine and Ohio about the graduation. They were so gracious and took vacation time to help me celebrate this special occasion. One friend in particular, Bart, played an integral role in me being able to attend my daughter's graduation. Bart, has a special place in my heart for how consistent he has been with his friendship. This man has driven all the way to Chicago just to celebrate my birthday. We lived in a predominately black area in Chicago; and with Bart being a tattooed and pierced Caucasian male, it took guts to even set foot in the neighborhood. Having Bart ride with me cut down the cost for me to see my oldest daughter graduate from the 8th grade. I didn't have the money for a plane ticket because the money I saved up was going to be used for my mother and daughter's plane tickets to see the progress I had made with Juice Express Eagles. I wanted to surprise them and reunite sisters that hadn't seen each other in a few years because of my mistakes.

On the way to the graduation, we decided to start recording our journey when we got to Akron, Ohio. Bart brought a video camera, we might as well use it. When we arrived in Chicago, my closest cousin Dro, showed us a great time. He had to work, but he got the "24 -hour flu" and called in sick. We went on a brief tour of Chicago and ate at a China town restaurant. It was pouring down rain so the tour got cut short.

The following morning, we drove from Dro's house to my old high school and videotaped my high school coach, whom I hadn't seen in over 20 years. We reminisced about my senior year in high school and the impact I made there. My notoriety as an elite basketball player was bred in that gymnasium. From there, I went to visit my father who stays in the Englewood nursing home in Chicago. It was great to see him and we had a nice visit. While we were there, we interviewed my pops about the effects that the stroke had on him and how his life has changed. After we left the nursing home, it was time to turn in. Pooh's special day was tomorrow!

It was going to be challenging to get to the graduation because we didn't know where the ceremony was being held. My name was not on the school's parent list so they couldn't disclose that information to me. My saving grace was the relationship I cultivated with some of the teachers at the front desk. They told me the location but broke the news to me that I wouldn't be able to enter without a ticket. Feeling a knot forming in my stomach, I hung up the phone and tears immediately ran down my face. There was a strong possibility I wouldn't see my daughter's proudest moment. Once a moment is missed, you never get it back and that hurt tremendously. Time is a currency that you can't earn back.

I was at my mother's house and I needed to be alone. I fell to my knees and whispered, *"Lord, I know you know my heart and what type of father I am to my daughters. If it's in your will, thy will be done."* I got up and got dressed and went back out in to the living room. My mother asked me, *"Are you ok?"* My heart was on my sleeve and the hurt on my face is transparent but I replied, *"Mom Dukes, it's in God's hands, no worries. If I have to stand outside of Miss Takila's graduation, so be it; but she will know that her daddy was there. No ticket won't stop me from seeing my daughter graduate."*

My mom let us use her car to save Bart money on gas. I grabbed the keys off of the table and started to walk to the car. My friends helped me carry my daughter's balloons, flowers and gifts. My friends were somewhat reluctant to get into the car and my mother looked concerned. No one had seen me drive for quite some time now. Bart took pictures of my "Cheshire Cat" smile because this was actually my first time driving a car since the stroke. It was an adjustment at first, but driving a car was similar to the riding a bike cliché. Good thing I got my driver's permit in Maine before I came to Chicago.

We arrived at the ceremony which happened to be right around the corner from where my daughter lives. We walked in to the church but were halted in our tracks because we didn't have tickets to get into the auditorium. My daughter and her classmates are standing so close, but yet so far away. I'm standing there looking in like I'm window shopping and one of the parents recognized me. *"You're Takila's daddy right? That is your twin! Why are you standing in the hallway when you should be in there in the ceremony?"* I replied back in a somber voice, *"I didn't get a ticket but me and my friend drove 2000 miles just to be here."* With an angry tone the parent says, *"Wait a damn minute, let me see if I can get my daughter to give you a ticket. Don't you worry, we will get you in!"* Someone was looking out for me that day, the teachers at the door overheard our conversation and gave all three of us tickets! I was so humbled by their act of kindness and thanked them. In an effort to not cause a scene, I took a seat at the back of the auditorium. I made it…*"Thank you Father, there is no problem too big for you,"* I thought to myself.

My daughter saw us walk in and the look on her face was priceless. She had no idea I was going to be in attendance. Bart videotaped most of the ceremony so that I could always have a hard copy of the graduation for my personal library. When the ceremony concluded we were the first to greet her outside. I gave my daughter her gifts, took pictures and told her how much I loved her. Her mother had a graduation party planned for Pooh, but of course I wasn't welcome. My plan was to have a barbeque at my mother's house for her graduation, but that was also out of the question. We ended up cooking for family and friends in place of the graduation party. All of my plans were ruined. No Maine trip for my daughter. No graduation party. Almost missed the graduation, I might as well cancel the tickets. We travelled so far and sacrificed so much; for such a short moment, but it was worth it.

Another journey to Chicago was coming to an end. The trip didn't go as planned, but the support and love from the family was priceless. We were on our way to the expressway, when a call came through on my phone. *"Where are you at Icepack?!"* I replied *"Almost by the e-way about to head back."* Dro's tone was urgent, almost frantic, *"Bro pull over meet me at the gas station on 71st and the Dan*

Ryan!" We detoured to the gas station to meet up and my cousin jumped out of the car with my brother "Mookie" to chastise me, "*Don't you ever do that again, you don't know when will be the last time we will see each other again!*" After a little conversation and a great big group hug, we went our separate ways. While we were riding back to Maine, the talk I had with Dro keeps replaying in my head. There was an eerie feeling I just couldn't shake. The night of September 23rd would provide clarity on how I was feeling.

On the outside of the ceremony looking in.

Dad and the happy graduate.

65

The disaster train was barreling down the track, full steam, with no way to stop the ensuing carnage. Searching for a suitable place to live on a fixed income was not getting me anywhere. Homeless and losing hope, a few good friends let me use their spare bedroom or couch so that I'd have a warm place to lay my head. I always made sure to contribute to the household in some way; whether it was paying rent or providing food.

During this time, I was juggling coaching my team and being there every day for my youngest daughter. I picked her up from school and made sure she completed her homework. Both of my daughters and I had phone bills that I paid for using my limited income. I never showed any worries until it got closer to the end of my stay in Maine. I tried everything in my power to stay; I even put my name on the shelter home list. The queue was so deep that I wasn't given the opportunity to get a bed. The stress was getting to me and I confided in some trusted associates.

Word got out around in my church about my situation and it was somewhat embarrassing. I would have preferred confidentiality in this case, but I only have myself to blame for the predicament I was in. Unsure of what my next move was going to be, I turned in for the night.

I was awakened from a deep slumber by my phone vibrating out of control. The constant buzz made me roll over to see what the commotion was. There were over 57 missed called and around 30 text messages. This was not an hour in which good news was typically the topic of conversation. I sat up and braced myself for whatever news I was about to receive. As I'm texting my mother, a restricted call comes through. It was my mother and she asked, *"Are you up?"* I replied *"Yes."* For some reason she repeated the question, *"Are you up?"* At this point, I'm getting upset because I know it's bad, I just didn't know how bad. She says to me, *"Yeah, you know Woodrow's dead?"* I said *"huh?!"* as I'm thinking it's my uncle Maine, who is also named Woodrow, I start to get butterflies in my stomach. Tearing up because I thought I lost my dear uncle my mother said, *"not your uncle, it's Dro."* I immediately lost it. *"What! Wait! No mama. No! I just talked to him! What happened to him?!"* My mother was weeping and she replied, *"He died in a car crash this morning."* I burst into tears and threw my phone. I was frantic and walked out of the house and screamed to the Heavens, *"No Lord! Why?! Why him?!"* I asked to go to the store to purchase the very thing that caused a lot of trouble in my life. I needed to numb the pain, although this wasn't the best way to go about it. But it didn't matter; my cousin, no, my brother, was no longer here! *"Ice don't you ever do that again, you never know if we will see each other again"* played over and over in my head. It was as if Dro was Machiavelli and predicted this ominous event.

I haven't felt this way since 1999, when I lost my grandmother and auntie. I was hoping this was a bad dream, that I would wake up at any moment and Dro would still be with us. He has three beautiful daughters that have to go through life without their father. It's time for the funeral and I am not ready to let go. I was in line to pay my respects, and when I got to the casket, I walked right past it without even taking a glimpse inside. I couldn't do it. My lifeless cousin was in a box. All I could do is give his mother a big hug and go downstairs in a futile attempt to run away from reality.

After reflecting alone for a while the mother of his child came to the back to check on me. She comes close to me to give me a hug and my heart was crumbling inside my chest. She says, *"Come on let me walk you up there,"* I reply *"I can't, but know this, I got you and the girls."* Then I went back downstairs. Every time I get thought I mustered up enough courage to walk up there to see him, I lost my nerve. Somebody comes downstairs and says *"Juice they are not going to close the casket until you come upstairs and see Dro."* I start making my way up to see him, but instead I went outside so I didn't have to see him. Gathering up my faux courage, I went to the casket. It felt like my legs were going to give out. My tears are flowing like the River Jordan and flash backs of our childhood are racing through my head. As the ushers make their way to the front to close the casket, I start to hyperventilate. Looking down on Dro for the final time, a part of me was waiting for him to get up.

He looked like he was fresh from the barbershop because his hairline was so crisp. They close the lid to the casket and I'm so distraught I forgot that I'm a pallbearer. I grab the right front-side of casket and take that long walk to the hearse. Tears rushed down my face and I tried to hide my shame so that everyone wouldn't see me. My auntie Georgia and my second mother Patty Cake wrapped me in their loving arms. I jumped in the car with 'Quick' who has always

68

been considered a brother. He is trying to talk to me but my mind was in another world. Quick watched his mother die right before his very eyes and he was sharing that traumatic experience.

We arrive at the cemetery and I was holding my emotions in check until the pastor uttered the words, *"ashes to ashes, dust to dust."* A part of me wanted my soul to leave with him, but I knew I have to grind even harder because a lot of people are counting on me. I lean all the way in the grave and tears are running down my eyes. My mother comes over and says *"I know that was your brother and I know it's hard, but he needs you to be strong and make sure his kids ok and I know you will." I didn't want to let him go but God makes no mistakes. He has a plan and sometimes we don't comprehend what it is. "* Death is a part of life that all of us will encounter someday. I had a massive brain hemorrhage that could have taken me out of here, but it wasn't my time. There is a greater plan for me, a purpose that is not yet fulfilled. When it's my time to take my final breath, I hope I make it to paradise.

Dro, my mother and I

The journey has been a long, hard road. I was blessed enough to beat death, and given a second chance at life. My travels have taken me to 49 of the 50 states, and in those 49 states I have visited at least 7 cities. Basketball was my profession for a short period of time, and I am forever thankful for the opportunity to be a semi-pro player. Maine and Texas have teams that I have started. Over forty kids that I have trained have received scholarships or have gone on to play college basketball. My face has been in magazines, television, newspapers and even on billboards. I have been fortunate enough to address mayors, city councils and senators. Why am I sharing this information? It's not to brag or boast ladies and gentlemen. It's to serve as an inspiration to let you know that what you believe, you can conceive.

Several of these accomplishments came AFTER I had my stroke and was labeled disabled. I was told I would be paralyzed; I'd never walk or talk. My mind said, *"No! You will do these things again!"* I spoke my destiny into existence. You can accomplish anything that you put your mind to, as long as you keep the faith and you put the work behind it! It's important to eliminate the distractions in your life and maintain a strong support system.

When I first set out on my journey, many doors were slammed in my face. I was physically weak and my brain capacity was definitely not the same. To this day, I still face challenges with my health, but a strong support system helped keep me going. I travelled to Sumter, South Carolina for two reasons. The first, was to visit family that is near and dear to my heart. The second, to leave distractions behind and work on my craft. My aunt Betty has always been a pillar in my life. If I ever want to learn about family history or need my spirit lifted, she's my go to. My cousin Priscilla, she has always treated me like one of her own. If I need a brutally honesty opinion or advice, she definitely is the one. There's never any love lost between us. Finally, my cousin Damien. I call him my little 'cuzzo' because we go way back. We can talk about any and everything. Months ago, I called him and talked about wanting to change my current situation for the better. "Let's build something that's ours, as a family," He said *"Let's get it! It's just you and me bro, if no one else believes in us or will help, that's okay."* He has been down with my vision since day one. After some deliberation, we decided the best move was to travel to Bowling Green, Ohio and finish what I started over three years ago.

On the way to Ohio, I fell very ill. Sickness hits me harder since I've had the stroke and I felt like death. Despite feeling as sick as I did, I never lost my drive to keep working on this project. Just when I thought I was in the clear, I had an episode. We were in a local grocery chain and pain ravaged my body. Sharp pains were shooting up my left side and it made me slump over my shopping cart. Damien was by my side ready to take me to the emergency room. I told him that I was fine, but nothing compared to Sept 2012. That experience changed me and made me want to get my story out there even more. I know my time is limited and I plan on using that time to inspire and motivate.

I'm still working with the American Heart Association and other organizations that help people that have disabilities like mine. Talking with the mother of my child, I find out more details of things that I have trouble recalling. For example, a month into my hospital stay, I had a port placed in my upper left chest to make it easier to give me medication without having to give me shots in my arms. *"You also have a stint placed in your right side of your neck to prevent any blood clots in the future,"* she told me. That's when I realized that my primary doctor didn't have as much knowledge of my treatment and condition as I had initially believed. I called every hospital trying to find out what went on with me while I was in the hospital, and it took the mother of one of my children to fill in the blanks.

Having to find out this way was very upsetting to me. To this day, I still have more questions than answers. The accounts of what I went through varies depending on who you ask. If you were in my shoes, wouldn't you want some sort of closure? I shouldn't have to chase people down to find out what happened to me in the hospital. People don't understand that although I was able to respond and hold conversations during my hospital stay, my memories are still hazy.

Communication sometimes is frustrating because people often forget that I'm still sick and don't know how my mind has been affected since they haven't experienced a stroke. It hurts my feelings when people treat me a certain way expecting the old me to respond; when in all actuality, I am a fraction of my former self. Just because it takes me a little longer to process information doesn't mean I'm dumb.

72

In fact, it doesn't mean that I can't do certain things either; such as write a memoir. I have dreams and aspirations and will pursue them, relentlessly, disability or not.

My path in life has been filled with obstacles, twists and turns. Knocking on death's door has drawn me closer to a higher power, and I am able to use my faith to better deal with adverse situations. The older version of myself would stress, get angry, act out, or grab a drink; which isn't necessarily the right way to deal with problems. I'm not a preacher, but I share my faith whenever someone needs it and is willing to listen. I'm far from perfect and am still learning and working on becoming a better man. It is my hope that people read these words and are inspired to do something for the better. Whether it's volunteering your time, spreading kindness with your words, or even making it right with that family member or friend you haven't seen eye to eye with. I realize that my time here is limited and I want to make the most of it. This is not a platform to bad-mouth or bash anyone; this is a memoir of a life changing event that tested my fortitude and faith, this is my story…*My Walking Testimony.*

On the way to Ohio, sick as a dog.

73

The following dialog contains grammatical and spelling errors. In order to maintain the integrity and emotion in each response, they have been printed as written by each respondent.

Takila

"…You are my back-bone, my spine, as a matter of fact you are my entire body because I would take a bullet for you. You are my only king and ever will. No other man can take your spot ever in life no matter if it's my boyfriend you will always be #1 on my list. God has given me an angel and a strong healthy man who cares and will do anything for his daughters even if it means going broke because you will always find a way. And I am very grateful for you being my father."

"…I wanted to cry when I went to the hospital. I prayed for him every night and crossed my fingers and it worked! A couple months later he was out of the hospital and I'm so, so, so happy he's with me right now because if he wasn't here I would or been more than balling but crying every single night but his soul would still protect me from the dangers and if you need to have someone to talk to he's the one. He's the best dad you could ever have and I love him dearly. I wouldn't trade my dad for anything not even the world."

In order to try and understand what my loved ones went through, I sent out a short questionnaire and asked them to respond in their own words. Here are some of the responses:

Questionnaire

1.On the day of Sept 26, 2012, where were you when you heard the news about me?

I was at my office working when I received a telephone call from my daughter, Kylee (Keyanna's Mom) about her needing to go Maine General Medical Center in Augusta, ASAP. While Juice was playing basketball at the YMCA, he had a stoke and the doctors didn't expect him to come out of it as his brain was hemorrhaging. Maine General Medical Center was trying to stabilize Juice, as they were going to transport him to Maine Medical Center in Portland as soon as this occurred. -CH

I was Just Coming Home From School When I Found Out. It Was A Day Late Though. -TM

On that day I was at home chilling when I received a call from K.Y. So I called the family to let them know what happened. After everyone received the news we all went to Anna Moore house an she wasn't their. We proceed to call her cell phone an it was no answer. After hours had passed those who were there was in a state of shock not knowing rather or not you would make it out of the comma. Anna had finally made it home an I had to be the one to break the terrible news. Of course it was a lot of crying an as she set on her couch continually blaming herself for what just happened to het son Antrone. Time had passed an K.Y. kept informing the family about everything that was going on with Antrone. Anna then stated that she needs to get where her son is, so we got her a plane ticket to Maine. Prayers went up an a blessing came down. Days had gone by an we received a phone call that Antrone has made it out of his comma an that he will not be the same. -MG

I was at work and saw on Facebook that you had been rushed to the hospital, I called my husband, Fredrick Evans,and asked if he had heard what happened,,,he had not, At that moment,I messaged a few people that had commented on the post to see what happened. One of those people was Kylee(whom I had never met before)she called me and explained that you had been at the gym and was rushed to the hospital and being sent to Maine Medical Center in Portland. I told her that me and my husband would go to MMC ASAP and meet her there. Kylee knew my husband but my first time meeting her was walking into the ICU at MMC.. When I walked in, she was in the hallway and we hugged and wiped each other's tears.

If you were in Maine what your reactions in the hospital?

Because Bill and I were taking care of Juice's daughter, and did not want her to be worried unnecessarily until it was known what was going to take place i.e., what they were going to do with her father; where her father was going to be, etc. etc. Our focus was totally on keeping Keyanna's life as normal as possible for her. We didn't want to have Keyanna afraid and scared by seeing her Dad with all kinds of hospital equipment on him. We wanted Keyanna's memories to be happy ones of her Dad. -CH

I couldn't believe my eyes. They filled with tears as I held your hand. I didn't know what to say so I just stared at you with my husband by my side. My husband kept shaking his head saying this was you, to pull through, I kept waiting for your response but there was no none,not even movement, J.E and F.E

If you were in Chicago and by my mother, what was her reaction?

I Wasn't Specifically By Her But I Know Her Reaction Was So Heart Broken, overwhelmed, and She Just cried and cried -TM

2.When you saw me for the first time, what was your reaction?

To be totally honest I would have to say that I had never had occasion to see anyone in the condition that Juice was in. I have been to see many, many people while they were hospitalized but Never had I seen so many pieces of equipment attached to a human's body as I did when I went to see Juice at Maine Medical Center in Portland. I had been warned by my daughter, Kylee, that it was not going to be pretty and had a forewarning, but still I was surprised at what I saw. Holes drilled in Juice's head, clear bags hooked to machinery with bloody matter coming from his brain, I cannot express the number of machines that were helping in keeping Juice alive. -CH

3.How was my physical appearance and mental state at the moment versus the Juice you knew before the stroke?

I honestly didn't think that Juice would come out of being in a coma, and even if he did come out of the coma, I never expected him to be able to know anyone, be able to speak so he could be understood, possibly never be able to walk and possibly not to know anyone that he knew before his stoke occurred. -CH

I was So Happy, Excited, Relieved And Joyful For Having My Father Back In My Life Because One Day He Is Goin To See Me Graduate College and High school. Also Maybe Might Even Become A Grandpa After I Finish School and I want him To Be part Of Their Lives, I want them To Know And Remember Him for A Wonderful Person nobody can ever ask for. -TM

You looked lifeless. You had tubes galore coming out of your head, throat, neck and arms. I remember thinking if you come out of this it will be a miracle! The atmosphere was quiet, all you heard was the beeping of medical equipment, This was NOT the Juice I knew! The Juice that was full of life, laughing an smiling making jokes every chance he got. The Juice I knew couldn't stay still...the "Juice" that was in front of me at the time was too still and unable to move. J.E and F.E

4.In your opinion, do you feel God spared my life?

Let me first say that I do believe in a higher power and I choose to call this higher power God. It is my belief that God did spare Juice's life, there is absolutely no question in my mind. I believe that God had additional plans and/or work for Juice to do before he gets his wings. I am sure that Juice would have wanted to go to meet his Granma and Auntie, whom he loves and misses so very much, but God was the one who decides what the plan of action will be, so Juice is still here on earth, walking, talking, playing basketball and loving life, more than ever.

I have told Juice during some discussions we've had after and during his recovery of what I have mentioned above, Juice knows how and what I believe. I have always reminded Juice that God had a plan for him and spared him his life and it is my hope and prayer that Juice never forgets what God did for him, he spared him his life.

My prayer is that Juice does God's work for the gift that he gave him. I want Juice to always remember that he received a second chance and most don't get that second chance in life. -CH

Yes! I Believe God Did Save My fathers life Because he Brought Him Back To Me And Still Wants Him To Be A Good Father To His Kids . God Is Saying It Isn't His Time Yet. -TM

YES! From Doctors telling you had 50/50 chance of living to a full recovery, playing ball and living life! Some said you'd never walk again, never playball again-and you used those words to prove them all wrong! J.E and F.E

Going through my emails and look what I find Wow Tears had forgot he answered questions before leaving this earth?

1.How was Juice mentally and physically before the stroke?2.what changed after the stroke?3, how was juice work ethic and attitude towards getting better? 4 what was your reaction to Juice stroke before and after? 5. What you think motivates Juice right now? 6 Do you feel God spared Juice life? Why? Why not? 1)He was on top of his game at his best 2)A lot changed he lost a lot of weight but his mind was still there same person different body structured but as far as talking lil slow at first but still it was him 3).he was sure of a speedy recovery he started getting into shape more running working on his muscles getting better eating habits got better.4)I was angry I was mad at the world I was devastated I didn't know what to do I thought I was losing someone who meant a lot to me didn't know exactly how to feel at the time didn't want to talk to anyone but I prayed to GOD that he would bring you back to me and God answered. God First his daughters his mom, family and friends. I would say he's very blessed always he'd made a incredibly progressive recovery faster than some and is the most motivated person I know.6) Yes I believe God gave him a second chance at life again and allow him to start over. Always my Best Friend Rest Easy #DROHOLIDAY

I don't remember the specific day you opened up but it was a week and three days after you had slipped into the coma, you were very confused, although you couldn't speak when you first opened your eyes but your eyes said it all because you were looking around you. The Doctors mentioned you would have short term memory loss, but that you would need lots of therapy to be able to speak and find words to express yourself. You had a infection and needed to bring your body temperature down. You had a fever for a couple of days and that it's a sign of infection, so they ran tests to find out where the infection was so they could treat it.so they ran all kind of blood work and tests. You had a drain put in your head on the left side to drain blood and fluid that was building up in your brain and to relieve pressure. You also had a port placed on the left upper chest to make it easier to give you medication without having to stick you in the arms. You also have a stint placed in your right side of your neck to prevent any blood clots in the future. You also had a feeding tube placed because you had lost so much weight and wasn't able to eat at the time for a long time. OH my goodness you had a tube coming out of your nose, one out of your head, one on each arm, a urine catheter and tubes coming out of your mouth. There were so many I can't begin to tell you. All the machines were doing something or it was giving you medicine. I filled out the forms because you had no family there at the time and I was next of kin and it was important because you were actively bleeding and your brain was swelling from the fluid and blood build up. If I hadn't signed the form and the drain didn't go in your head, there was no chance of survival and the doctor told me that face to face.K.B.

Email questionnaire

> 1) What was the first day I opened my eyes?What did I do? Was I confused?

I don't remember the specific day that you opened up your eyes for the first time but it was about a week and three days after you had slipped

into the coma. Yes you were very confused, although you couldn't speak when u first opened your eyes but your eyes said it all because you kept just looking around you.
>
> 2)What did the doctor's say Could possibly happen if I ever was going to wake up?

The doctors mentioned that you were going to have some short term memory loss, but that you would know who we were but you would need lots of therapy to be able to speak and find the words to express yourself.

> 3)Why was it necessary for the IcePack to be put under my arms and private parts?

You had an infection and needed to bring your body temperature down. You had a fever for a couple of days and that is a sign of infection, so they ran all kinds of blood work and tests to find out where the infection was so that they could treat it.
> 4)Did I have other surgeries or procedures done when I was in the hospital?

You had the drain put in your head on the left side to drain blood and fluid that was building up in your brain and to relieve pressure. You also had a port placed on the left upper chest to make it easier to give you medication without having to stick you in the arms. You also have a stint placed in your right side of your neck to prevent any blood clots in the future. You also had a feeding tube placed because u had lost so much weight and wasn't able to eat at the time for a long time.

> 5)How many people was allowed in the ICU Unit at a time and how would you all alternate?

There was only supposed to be immediate family only, but they were very good about letting other people in to visit if your mother and I said it was alright. They only allowed 3 people in there at a time because there were so many machines and lines and equipment and you were very ill.

> Did you witness someone in Unit Passing away? How did that make

you feel about my chances of survival?

No, thankfully I did not witness any deaths on the Unit while you were there but to be honest, I wasn't focused on anyone else around me other than you. I prayed a lot hoping that God would give u another chance at life, but honestly you had a 50/50 chance of living.

> 6)When I was placed on the General floor in Maine Meds was my I in the clear or was it some other obstacles?

When u were finally placed on the general floor there were still some obstacles that you had to deal with...the first one being your meds. You weren't thinking clearly and still not able to get up on your own, feed yourself or talk clearly.

> 7)Did the Doctor's or Nurse's indicate to you that I would walk again?

They told me that the only good thing going for you is that you were young. They asked me if you were the type of person who would be determined to walk again and if so, then it would happen but only after a lot of hard work and dedication.

> 8)When did you put the picture of Fred Sanford up and Why?lol

My mother printed that off because she wanted you to be in good spirits. We wanted to make you smile when u woke up and know that we all love you. I think she put that up a couple days after u woke up from the coma.

> 9)What was my mood swings while you all visit?

You had good and bad days and moments. Sometimes you would just start to cry, and this is when u couldn't even talk. I would wipe your tears and say that your fine and everything is gonna be ok. I hated to see you cry and frustrated so I used to tell u that if you were gonna cry then I was going to leave. I remember one time I showed u pics of keke to make you smile and you broke down crying. I told you that she is fine and I wanted to share what a happy child we have..didn't want u to cry.

> 10)How many wires would you estimate that I had on my brain and body and why was all the machines hook up to me?

Oh my goodness, you had a tube coming out of your nose, one out of your head, one on each arm, a urine catheter and then tubes coming out of your mouth, I want to say three in your mouth. There were so many I can't even begin to tell you. All the machines were doing something different, whether it was draining something or it was giving you medicine.

> 11)Who filled out the form?Why was it necessary to do this procedure? (Question for Ky) Thank You for it in advance have a Great Weekend

I filled out the forms because you had no family here at the time and it was important because you were actively bleeding and your brain was swelling from the fluid and blood build up. If I hadn't signed the form and the drain didn't go in your head, there was no chance of survival and the doctor told me that face to face.

Uncle Leon response:
In response to the first question: Juice was physically and mentally fit and a well rounded individual. two: After the stroke Juice's speech was somewhat incoherent and his physical acumen was erratic and he had to be helped to stand and walk. He also lost a lot of weight which made him weak and listless. Juice made a miraculous comeback from the stroke. Despite his physical disability, he was able to overcome his shortcomings and began to train, nourish, and will his body into the condition in which he enjoys today. Juice understood that he had made a miraculous recovery from the stroke due to the Grace of God. He is totally aware of this fact and he shares his story with everyone. He expresses his belief in God daily. Juice eagerly tries to help others and has started an organization which includes children, who he tries to help and develop using basketball as a tool. To thank God for this miraculous gift Juice devotes most of his time sharing, caring, and teaching his two daughters and the children of others who have placed them under his tutelage. three: Juice was totally committed to getting better after his unfortunate stroke. He complied with the treatment and

suggestions outlined by his physicians and was always in prayer with the Lord. He became a man on a mission to spread the word using his comeback from the stroke to teach others a better way. His can do attitude is infectious. four: I was shocked to find out that Juice had a stroke. He was physically active and I thought was in good condition and I knew of no others in our family that had a heart condition. five: What drives Juice today, I believe is his Gift of a second chance at life from God almighty. All of us were put here for a reason and I believe God wasn't finished with Juice or he has not fulfilled his God given purpose here on earth. I believe this is the spark which burns in Juice's heart and drives him daily to express his love and devotion to God by telling his story.

Photo Gallery

Acknowledgements:

Juice-I want to thank God, first and foremost. He is the head of my life and guides me. I want to acknowledge the pillars in my family that have paved the way. May they rest easy. Special acknowledgment to the following that are no longer here physically, but are always with me in spirit. Thank you Grandma Lucy Lee Spencer Williams, Auntie Shirley "Pookie" Williams and Woodrow "Dro" Lawrence Williams Jr, Martell Lawrence, Michael Joseph, Mama Angie Evans, Uncle Willie Spencer, Sr, cousin Michael Spencer, my mentor and Coach Garland Dildy, my step dad Kempton Murray, Grandma Best Friend I.V. To all of you and a host of others, Rest in Heaven. My precious daughter's, Takila "Pooh Bear" Moore and Keyanna "Princess Keke" Moore for being the motivation for me to fight for my life. My late grandmother told me my work wasn't done. I want to personally thank Damien for the help and support he has given me in this project. No matter what time he had to work, he stayed up late with me, giving his input and adding flavor to this book. I want to personally thank Mom Dukes (Anna Moore) and my Pops (Howard Moore Sr.) for bringing me in this world. Without you, none of this would be possible. I love y'all to death. I hope you guys are proud of me!!! To both mothers of my children. Thank you for blessing this world with talented and beautiful children. It may not have worked out between us, but we can say we shared some unforgettable moments.

To my family and friends, I want to extend my sincerest thanks to all of you for being in my life. There are way too many of you to name, but know that you are in my thoughts and on my heart. Each of you have played an integral part in me becoming the man I am today.

To the medical staffs of Maine Medical Center, Thayer Hospital and Maine General Hospital, thank you for the medical attention, therapy, pushing me and most important, saving my life.Dr. Sedar thank you for doing the operation on me. Dr. Jerald Hurdle and Family, thank you immensely for what you did for me. I will never forget it, because without you, none of this would be possible. Special Thanks to Brooke Holycross for coming aboard and supporting from day one. I knew you would be special in my life and I would not have connected with you if it wasn't for you believing in and managing the next up and coming RnB singer, my cuzzo, Karlos Farrar! Thank you so much 2016 #YearofChanges

Damien-I would like to thank my mother Priscilla Womack, my parents Rev. Nathaniel Womack, Sr. and Tonia Womack. My grandmother Betty Spencer for being my rock. My kids Jamovia and Nairobi, daddy loves you! Cyla of course, special thanks. The Waheed women (can't take you anywhere!) My brothers and sisters: Bria, Kyra, Yalandria (Trish), Nate Jr, Corey, Eddie, Yvonne, Victoria, Aaron and your families. Uncle Duke and Family (Aunt Allison, Karlos, Alicia). Bryant, Chynalinn, Rodney, Rhonda much love. The Hamiltons, Logwoods, Moores, Spencers, Womacks, Browns, Ruffins family trees. I would like to acknowledge some of my friends that have been there for me, even in my dark times. Jen, Katelyn, Matt, Katy, Jakob (Jake), Jill, The Kellermeier family, Lurch, Hines-arelli, Willy, Chris, Jeremy "Rod", Dustin, The Hines family, The Cravenors, RIH to one of my best friends, Rob Cravenor. The Briggs family, The Kirian family, Cathy, David Hammer, Seth Ream and family, Jen T, Leah, Hannah, Emily K, Angela, John S, AJ aka Twon Don, Leslie C, Eric Himes, The Breakfast Club (Ashley, Linden, Tammy and Tammy aka "TNT"), Brenda Young, Trevis Reid, A-Rizzy, and Paco. To all my family, friends and associates, thank you for being there, I only had so many characters so know that you are on my mind and heart. #TeamHOW

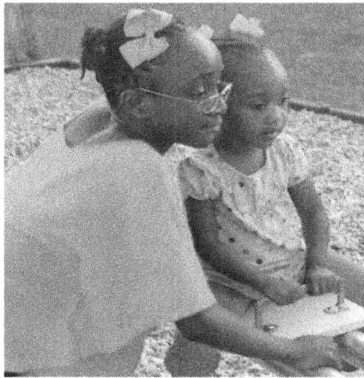

Daddy loves you Jamovia and Nairobi

R.I.H. Dr. Robert A. Cravenor July 18, 1981 – October 9, 2012

About the Authors

Antrone 'Juice' Moore is a graduate of University of Maine of Augusta. While attending the university he garnered Division II All-America honors. His talent allowed for his basketball career to continue post-collegiately in the semi-pro ranks; playing for teams such as the Lake County Lakers and the Harlem Ambassadors. Most important, he is a devoted father and family oriented. A firm believer in it is better to give than to receive. Wherever he takes up residence, he looks for volunteer opportunities to be a community activist to help service the community. Antrone is CEO of Juice Express Eagles a certified AAU youth basketball team which teaches basketball skills to numerous age groups, boys and girls, with the goal to teach them not only on court skills, but life lessons. In his spare time, he volunteers for the Heart and Stroke Associations. In the state of Maine, he makes sure to give back through his work as a Peer Navigator for Maine General. "Take it to the Rim" basketball clinics were also established by Juice with the goal of teaching kids the proper fundamentals of the game. His love of the game lead to volunteer coaching gigs and eventually having his own AAU team; Juice Express Eagles of Augusta, Maine. Juice also founded an organization called H.O.W. or Helping Others Win.

Damien Womack is a 1999 graduate of Bowling Green State University. He has two beautiful daughters that are his shining stars. Family and friends are very important and a driving force to work hard. Damien helped with this project for the love of new challenges. He is the other founder of the organization H.O.W. Just a regular guy trying to do extraordinary things. In his spare time, he enjoys travel, reading and sports. His motto is "Do

something different every day." Damien still resides in
Bowling Green, Ohio.

Striving for greatness

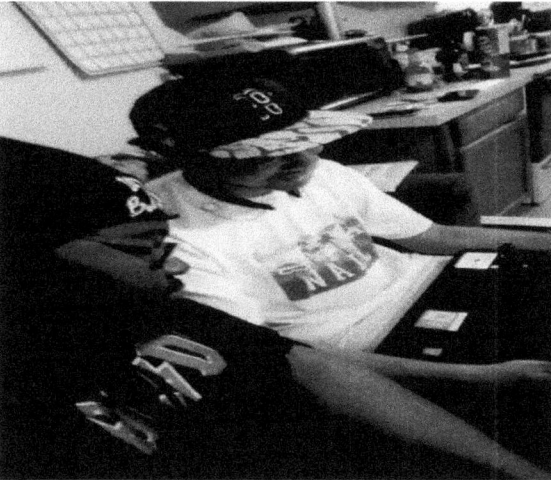

Putting the finishing touches on the project

www.ingramcontent.com/pod-product-compliance
Lightning Source LLC
Chambersburg PA
CBHW062009040426
42447CB00010B/1978